nickelodeon™

TEENAGE MUTANT NINJA™

TURTLES

DONNIE'S ROBOT

Popcorn
ELT
Readers

Meet ...
everyone from

These are the Teenage Mutant Ninja Turtles.
They live under New York City.

Leonardo

This is Leo. He is
the leader.

Raphael

This is Raph.
He is strong.

Michelangelo

This is Mikey.
He is funny!

Donatello

This is Donnie.
He is clever.

Splinter

This is Splinter. The
Turtles learn ninjutsu
from Splinter.

bo staff

The Kraang

The Kraang are aliens. They live inside Kraangdroids.

The Kraang make mutagen. Mutagen is dangerous.

mutagen

A Kraangdroid is a robot.

WATCH OUT! The Kraang are bad!

April

This is April. She is looking for her dad. The Kraang have got him.

Before you read ...
What do you think? Who are stronger? The Turtles or the Kraang?

New Words

What do these new words mean? Ask your teacher or use your dictionary.

city

It's a big **city**.

awesome

This is **awesome**!

fight

The boys are **fighting**. They're having a **fight**.

brave

She's **brave**!

fire

The alien **fired** at the people.

hit

Hit it!

remote control

This is a **remote control**.

warehouse

What's in this **warehouse**?

pillar

The room has six **pillars**.

'Watch out!'

Watch out!

push

She's **pushing** her brother.

Verbs

Present	Past
fall	fell
hear	heard
win	won

CHAPTER ONE
A new idea

'Donnie! Watch out!' shouted Leo.

There was one last Kraangdroid, and it was in front of Donnie.

'Aaaarrr!' Donnie shouted. He hit the Kraangdroid with his bo staff. The Kraangdroid looked at him.

'I've got it!' Raph shouted. He ran at the Kraangdroid and it fell down. The Kraang alien jumped out and ran away.

Donnie looked at his bo staff.

'This thing is not cool,' he said. 'How can I fight the Kraang with an old bo staff?'

Then he looked at the Kraangdroid. 'I've got an idea,' he said.

'What are you doing, Donnie?' said Raph.

Donnie had one of the Kraangdroids. 'What's inside this thing?' he asked.

'There's a pink Kraang inside,' said Raph. 'You hit it and it jumps out!'

'I want to find out more,' said Donnie. 'Let's take it back home.'

The Turtles went back home. Donnie worked on the Kraangdroid. Splinter came to see.

'Sensei,' said Donnie. 'This robot is awesome! Please can I make something new from it?'

'Yes, of course,' said Splinter. 'Ninjas are clever and they like new ideas.'

'But fighting is not a computer game!' said Splinter. 'Are you listening, Donatello?'

'Thanks, Sensei!' said Donnie and he walked out of the room with the Kraangdroid.

'A computer game ...' he said quietly. 'That's a great idea!'

CHAPTER TWO
Donnie's robot

CRASH! BANG!

'What's that noise?' asked Mikey.

A robot walked into the room. It was small with blue eyes.

'Meet my new robot,' Donnie said.

'I love it!' said Mikey.

'It's very small,' said Raph.

'I've got a remote control,' said Donnie. 'Now I can stay at home and fight!'

'Ninjas don't stay at home!' said Leo.

'What does it do?' asked Raph.

'Fight it and see!' said Donnie.

'I don't want to break it!' laughed Leo.

'Aaaarrr!' shouted Raph. He ran at the robot. The robot pushed him away.

'Easy!' said Donnie.

Now Mikey and Leo ran at the robot. The robot won again.

'Now who's laughing?' said Donnie.

'Can my robot go up to the city?' Donnie asked Splinter.

'Yes, it can,' said Splinter. 'But ... listen to me, Donatello. A new robot can't win a fight. Only YOU can win a fight. Ninjas must be brave.'

'OK, Sensei,' said Donnie.

CHAPTER THREE
Stop the Kraang!

April came to see the Turtles.

'Look!' she said. 'I found these pictures on the Internet.'

'It's a Kraang!' said Leo.

'Where?' shouted Mikey.

'It's not here! It's in a warehouse in the city,' said April. 'I'm going to find it. Are you coming?'

'No,' said Leo. 'It's daytime. Ninjas go out when it's dark.'

'I'm going now,' said April. 'Maybe my dad is there.'

April looked through the doors of the warehouse. She could see two robots. 'That's the Kraang!' said April quietly.

'Do you have the mutagen?' said one Kraangdroid. 'We can put the mutagen in the water of this city.'

'Yes,' said the other Kraangdroid. 'Many people drink the water. There are going to be many new mutants!'

'Oh no!' thought April. 'I have to talk to the Turtles.' But April moved and the Kraang heard her. April was very frightened. 'What am I going to do?' she thought.

Then April thought of her friends, the Turtles. 'Think ninja!' she said quietly. She looked around and saw a small door.

When the Kraang came to find April, she was not there.

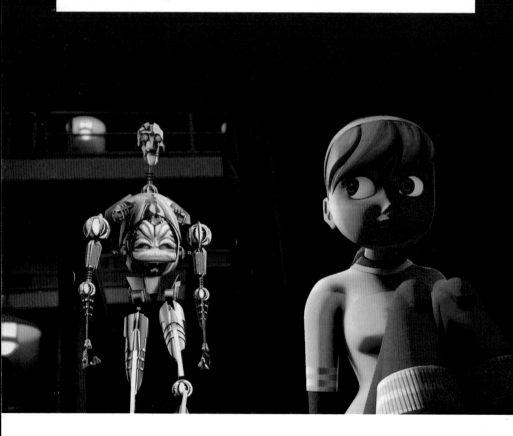

April found the Turtles in the city.

'The Kraang are putting mutagen into the water,' she said. 'We have to stop them!'

CRASH! BANG!

'What's that noise?' asked April. Then she saw Donnie's robot.

'It's Donnie's new idea,' said Leo.

'But it's quieter than Donnie!' laughed Raph.

Donnie was at home with the remote control. He talked through the robot. 'This is great!' said Donnie's robot. 'You're out in the cold and I'm here. And I'm eating Mikey's pizza!'

'Hey!' said Mikey.

'Let's go to the warehouse!' said Leo. 'But Donnie, you can't come!'

'Why not?' said Donnie's robot.

'You're too noisy!' said Leo. 'Ninjas are quiet!'

CHAPTER FOUR
'Donnie's here!'

The three Turtles went into the warehouse. April waited outside with Donnie's robot.

'I hope they're OK,' said Donnie's robot.

Then they heard Mikey. 'HELP!' he shouted.

'I'm going in!' said Donnie's robot.

Donnie's robot jumped into the warehouse. There were Kraangdroids everywhere! The Kraangdroids fired at Donnie's robot. They fired and fired. But the robot didn't fall.

'Now me!' shouted Donnie. Donnie's robot fired back. He was fast and strong and he won easily!

But Donnie couldn't stop. 'I love this!' he shouted. He fired again and again. Suddenly the robot stopped moving.

'There's a problem with the remote control!' shouted Donnie.

A Kraang jumped onto the robot's head.

'What's that Kraang doing?' asked Donnie.

The Kraang put its arms around the robot. Then the robot's eyes went pink.

'Stop the Turtles!' said the robot. Donnie's robot was now a Kraangdroid and it was in front of the Turtles.

'Run!' shouted Donnie, but the Turtles could not run.

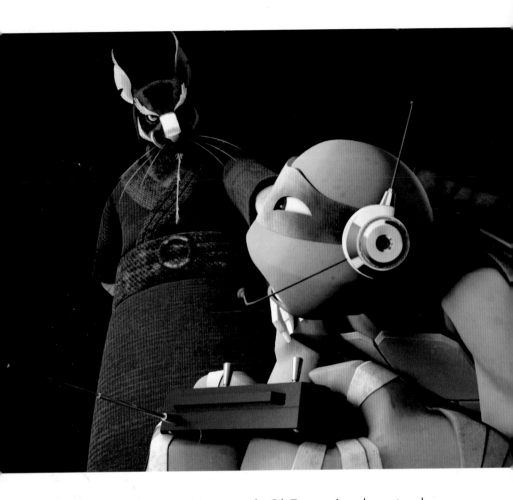

'What am I going to do?' Donnie shouted.

Suddenly Splinter was behind him. 'This is not a game now,' he said. 'Your brothers need you.'

'You're right, Sensei,' said Donnie and he ran to help.

'Wait, Donatello!' said Splinter. 'You are going to need this.' It was Donnie's bo staff.

'Thanks, Sensei!' said Donnie.

Donnie jumped into the warehouse.

'Yes!' shouted Mikey. 'Donnie's here!'

'You fight the Kraangdroids!' shouted Donnie. 'I'm going to stop the robot.'

But nothing stopped this robot. Donnie started to think. He saw a pillar next to him. The pillar was not very strong.

'I've got an idea,' he said.

Donnie jumped over the robot and pushed the pillar. The pillar hit the robot and the robot fell onto Donnie's bo staff.

'Stop ... the ... Turtles ...' said the robot slowly. The pink light in the robot's eyes went out.

'That was awesome, Donnie!' said Mikey.

But Raph wasn't happy. 'Why did you make that robot?' he said. 'It was a bad idea!'

Back home, Donnie was very quiet.

'Why are you sad?' asked Splinter.

'That was dangerous for the Turtles,' said Donnie. 'And it was all because of me.'

'Yes, it was,' said Splinter. 'But, thanks to you, we also stopped the Kraang and helped the people of this city!'

Now Donnie was happy. 'I don't need a robot!' he laughed. 'I'm a brave ninja!'

THE END

OUR ROBOT FRIENDS

snacks

There are many robots in the world today. They are all very different, but they all help people.

Meet Snackbot. Snackbot works at Carnegie Mellon University in Pittsburgh in the USA. When students at the university are hungry, Snackbot brings them a snack!

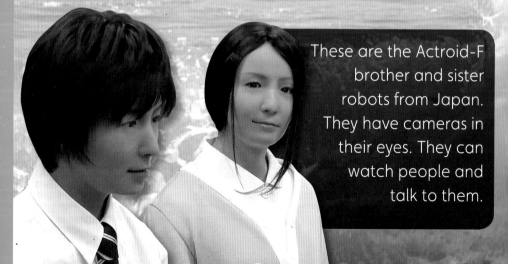

These are the Actroid-F brother and sister robots from Japan. They have cameras in their eyes. They can watch people and talk to them.

26

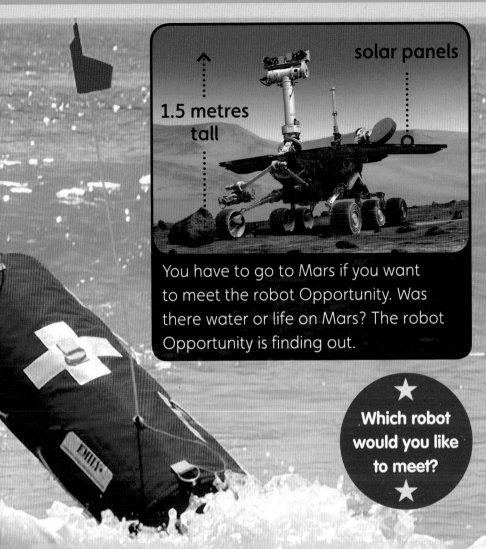

solar panels

1.5 metres tall

You have to go to Mars if you want to meet the robot Opportunity. Was there water or life on Mars? The robot Opportunity is finding out.

★ Which robot would you like to meet? ★

E.M.I.L.Y. does not look like a friend, but this robot helps people all the time. E.M.I.L.Y. works in Los Angeles in the USA. She rescues people from the sea. She swims faster than a person and can go out in strong winds.

What do these words mean? Find out.
camera   life   rescue   swim

After you read

1 **How much can you remember? Answer the questions.**

a) What colour are the Kraang? ......pink......

b) What colour are Raph's eyes? ....

c) Leo's eye mask is blue.
What colour is Donnie's? ....

d) Donnie's robot has blue eyes. What colour
are its eyes at the end of the story? ....

2 **Where did these events happen? Write W for warehouse or H for the Turtles' home.**

a) Donnie made a new robot. H

b) The Kraang heard April. ☐

c) Donnie's robot fired at the Kraang. ☐

d) April found some pictures of a Kraang on
the Internet. ☐

e) Donnie's robot pushed Raph away. ☐

f) Donnie stopped the robot. ☐

Where's the popcorn?
Look in your book.
Can you find it?

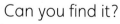

Puzzle time!

1 What do we learn about ninjas in the story? Complete the sentences.

1 They are c l e v e r .

2 They go out when it's d __ __ k.

3 They are b __ __ v __ .

4 They don't s __ __ y at home.

5 They are q u __ e __ .

2 Circle the odd one out.

a)

b)

c)

d)

3 Look at the pictures and do the crossword.

4a Did you like the story? Write your name in box 1 and colour the stars. Now ask five friends.

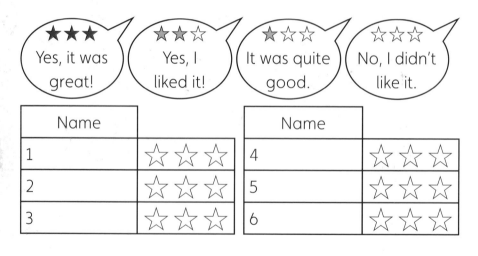

★★★
Yes, it was great!

★★☆
Yes, I liked it!

★☆☆
It was quite good.

☆☆☆
No, I didn't like it.

Name				Name		
1	☆	☆	☆	4	☆ ☆ ☆
2	☆	☆	☆	5	☆ ☆ ☆
3	☆	☆	☆	6	☆ ☆ ☆

b Complete the sentence with *everyone, some of us* or *no one*.

.... liked the story.

1 You are April. You are at the warehouse. Tell your story.

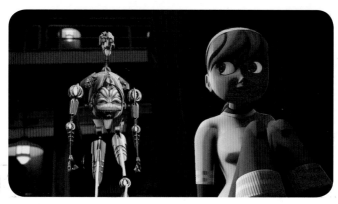

2 What do you think? How does April run away from the Kraangdroids? In pairs, think of an ending to her story.

Chant

1 🔊 **Listen and read.**

WATCH OUT!

It's small and makes
A lot of noise.
What's that?
It's Donnie's robot.

It wins the fight
It's fast and strong.
What's that?
It's Donnie's robot.

It's got pink eyes
And a Kraang on top.
What's that?
It's Donnie's robot!
WATCH OUT!

2 🔊 **Say the chant.**